The Complete French Home Cookbook

Simple French Recipes That Look Hard But Are Actually Not

BY

Jenny Kings

Copyright 2024 Jenny Kings.

License Notes

No part of this Book can be reproduced in any form or by any means including print, electronic, scanning or photocopying unless prior permission is granted by the author.

All ideas, suggestions and guidelines mentioned here are written for informative purposes. While the author has taken every possible step to ensure accuracy, all readers are advised to follow information at their own risk. The author cannot be held responsible for personal and/or commercial damages in case of misinterpreting and misunderstanding any part of this Book

Table of Contents

Introduction 6

Appetizers 8

   1. Classic French Onion Soup (Soupe à l'Oignon) 9

   2. Escargots de Bourgogne 12

   3. Quiche Lorraine 15

   4. Gougères 18

   5. Smoked Salmon Canapés 21

   6. Pâté en Croûte 24

   7. Coquilles Saint-Jacques 27

   8. Ratatouille Tartlets 30

   9. Foie Gras on Brioche 33

   10. Cheese and Charcuterie Board 36

Main Courses 40

   11. Boeuf Bourguignon 41

   12. Coq au Vin 44

   13. Duck Confit (Confit de Canard) 48

14. Bouillabaisse 51

15. Cassoulet 54

16. Steak au Poivre 58

17. Sole Meunière 61

18. Herb-Crusted Lamb Rack (Carré d'Agneau) 64

19. Ratatouille 67

20. Salmon en Croûte (Saumon en Croûte) 70

Sweets 73

21. Classic Crème Brûlée 74

22. Chocolate Soufflé 77

23. Upside-Down Apple Pie (Tarte Tatin) 80

24. Macarons 83

25. Profiteroles 87

26. Madeleines 91

27. Éclairs 94

28. Crêpes Suzette 97

29. Christmas Log Cake (Yule Log) 100

30. Clafoutis 104

Drinks 107

    31. Classic Mimosa 108

    32. Kir Royale 110

    33. French 75 112

    34. Vin Chaud 114

    35. Pastis 117

    36. Cognac 119

    37. Lumiere - A Gin Cocktail 121

    38. Calvados Sidecar 123

    39. Café au Lait 125

    40. Hot Chocolate (Chocolat Chaud) 127

Conclusion 129

Author's Afterthoughts 130

Introduction

Welcome to the world of French cooking made simple!

Many people think French food is too hard to make at home - but that's not true at all. French cooking is really about taking good ingredients and treating them with care to make something wonderful. It's about techniques that have been passed down through generations, made easier for today's home cooks.

In this book, we've taken classic French recipes and broken them down into clear, easy-to-follow steps. Whether you're making a warm onion soup on a cold day or baking a delicate pastry for dessert, you'll find that French cooking isn't as hard as you might think. Each recipe comes with helpful tips and tricks that we've learned from years of making these dishes.

You'll find recipes for everything from quick weeknight dinners to impressive party dishes. We've included the stories behind many dishes too - like how Tarte Tatin was invented by accident, or why French onion soup became a late-night favorite in Paris.

The best part? You don't need fancy equipment or hard-to-find ingredients. Most recipes use things you can get at your local grocery store. And don't worry if you make mistakes - that's how everyone learns! Each recipe includes notes about what might go wrong and how to fix it.

So roll up your sleeves, turn on your stove, and get ready to cook some amazing French food. These recipes have stood the test of time because they're just that good. Now it's your turn to make them in your own kitchen!

Let's start cooking!

Appetizers

1. Classic French Onion Soup (Soupe à l'Oignon)

This warm and rich soup started in Paris. French people love it so much they eat it late at night after parties. Sweet onions cooked in butter make the soup super tasty, and melted cheese on top makes it perfect for cold days. If you like cheese and onions, you'll want to make this again and again.

Preparation Time: 15 minutes

Cooking Time: 50 minutes

Serving Size: 4 servings

Ingredients:

- 4 slices of provolone cheese
- 4 slices of french bread
- 5 cups beef broth
- 1/4 cup grated Parmesan cheese
- 4 cups sliced onions
- 2 slices Swiss cheese, diced
- 2 tablespoons olive oil
- 2 tablespoons dry sherry
- 1/2 cup unsalted butter
- 1 teaspoon dried thyme
- Salt and pepper to taste

Instructions:

   a. Get everything ready on your counter.
   b. Put a big pot on medium heat. Drop in the butter and olive oil.
   c. Once the butter melts, add your sliced onions. Keep stirring them until they turn see-through and soft. Don't let them turn brown!
   d. Pour in the beef broth and sherry. Add thyme, salt, and pepper.
   e. Let everything bubble gently for 30 minutes.
   f. Turn on your oven's broiler.
   g. Pour the hot soup into oven-safe bowls.
   h. Put a slice of French bread on each bowl of soup. You can break the bread if it's too big.
   i. Layer the cheeses: first provolone, then Swiss, and finish with Parmesan on top.
   j. Put the bowls on a baking sheet and slide them under the broiler. Watch them carefully! Cook for 2-3 minutes until the cheese gets bubbly and a little brown.
   k. Serve right away while the cheese is still stretchy!

Special Notes:

- Cut your onions into same-size slices (about 1/4 inch thick) so they cook evenly. If they're too thin, they'll disappear in the soup.
- Try adding a splash of Worcestershire sauce (about 1 teaspoon) to the broth. It gives the soup an extra rich flavor that most people love!

2. Escargots de Bourgogne

This classic French appetizer has been around since forever. If you've never tried snails, this is your chance! They're cooked in a super tasty garlic-parsley butter that's so good, you'll want to soak up every last drop with bread. Trust me, it's not as weird as it sounds - the French can't be wrong about this one!

Preparation Time: 5 minutes

Cooking Time: 10 minutes

Serving Size: 24 snails (serves 4-6 as appetizer)

Ingredients:

- 24 empty snail shells
- 1 pinch black or white pepper, freshly cracked
- 1 can snails (escargots)
- 1 baguette, warmed and sliced
- 1 small shallot
- 2 large cloves garlic
- 1/4 cup fresh Italian parsley
- 1/4 cup (2 oz) salted butter, softened
- 1 tablespoon dry white wine

Instructions:

a. Clean those shells! Boil them in a big pot of water for 5 minutes.
b. Take them out, drain, and let them dry in the air. Turn your oven on to 400°F.
c. Time for the magic butter! Chop up the shallot, garlic, and parsley really fine.
d. Mix them with your soft butter, wine, and pepper until everything's well combined. If you're feeling fancy, put this mixture in a piping bag.
e. Get your snails ready by draining and rinsing them from the can.
f. Now for the fun part! Put some of your butter mix in each shell, pop in a snail, and cover it with more butter. You want those snails swimming in that good stuff!
g. Line up your filled shells in a baking dish, butter side up. Pack them close so they don't roll around. A mini muffin tin works great too!
h. Bake for 10 minutes until you see the butter bubbling and melted.
i. Get them while they're hot! Serve right away with your sliced baguette.

Special Notes:

- Add a tiny splash of Pernod or any anise-flavored liquor to the butter mixture. It adds this amazing subtle flavor that makes people go "Hmm, what IS that?"
- No shells? No problem! You can make this in small ramekins or even a mini muffin tin. Just skip the shell-cleaning step and put the butter, snail, and more butter directly in each cup. Works just as well!

3. Quiche Lorraine

Born in the Lorraine region of France, this savory pie has become a breakfast favorite worldwide. It's basically eggs, cream, and bacon wrapped in a buttery crust - what's not to love? The Swiss cheese makes it rich and melty, while the bacon adds a perfect salty crunch.

Preparation Time: 15 minutes

Cooking Time: 55 minutes

Additional Time: 10 minutes

Serving Size: 6 servings

Ingredients:

- 12 slices bacon
- 1 cup Swiss cheese, shredded
- 4 large eggs, beaten
- 3/4 teaspoon salt
- 1/4 teaspoon white sugar
- 1/8 teaspoon cayenne pepper
- 1/3 cup onion, minced
- 1 (9-inch) pie crust
- 2 cups light cream

Instructions:

Get your oven hot - set it to 425°F.

Cook the bacon first:

a. Put it in a big pan
b. Cook until brown and crispy (about 10 minutes)
c. Drain on paper towels
d. Chop it up into bits

Layer your pie:

a. Put the bacon pieces in the pie crust
b. Add the Swiss cheese
c. Sprinkle the minced onion

Mix the wet stuff:

   a. In a bowl, beat together cream, eggs, salt, sugar, and cayenne
   b. Pour it over everything in the pie crust

Two-step baking:

   a. First 15 minutes at 425°F
   b. Then turn down to 300°F
   c. Keep baking about 30 more minutes
   d. It's done when you stick a knife near the edge and it comes out clean

Let it rest 10 minutes before cutting.

Special Notes:

- Try warming your eggs and cream to room temperature before mixing. This helps everything cook more evenly and makes the filling extra smooth.
- Want to change it up? Add 1/4 cup of chopped fresh mushrooms with the onions. They add an earthy flavor that goes great with the bacon and cheese.

4. Gougères

These small, airy cheese puffs come from France. They're like mini cheese clouds that melt in your mouth. Made with basic ingredients like butter, flour, eggs, and Gruyère cheese, they're perfect for parties or as a quick snack. People love them because they're light but packed with cheese flavor.

Preparation Time: 20 minutes

Cooking Time: 25 minutes

Cooling Time: 30 minutes

Serving Size: 20 puffs

Ingredients:

- 1 cup all-purpose flour, sifted
- 4 large eggs
- 1 cup water or milk
- 6 tablespoons unsalted butter, cut into small cubes
- 1/2 teaspoon salt
- 1 cup Gruyère cheese, finely grated, plus extra for topping
- 1 pinch nutmeg
- 1 pinch black pepper

For brushing:

- 1 large egg mixed with 1 tablespoon water (or cooking spray)

Instructions:

a. Put water (or milk), butter, and salt in a pot. Turn heat to high and cook until the butter melts and the liquid boils.
b. Take the pot off the heat. Add all the flour at once and stir hard until you don't see any flour lumps.
c. Put the pot back on medium-high heat. Keep stirring until the dough feels hot (175°F) and forms a ball.
d. Let the dough cool down to 145°F. You can either:
   - Put it in a stand mixer and beat until it cools down, or
   - Keep it in the pot and stir by hand until it cools
e. Add eggs one at a time. Mix each egg completely before adding the next one.

f. Mix in the cheese, nutmeg, and pepper.

g. Heat your oven to 400°F. Line a baking sheet with parchment paper.

h. Put the dough in a pastry bag. Pipe 1 1/2-inch rounds onto the baking sheet.

i. Smooth any pointy tips with a wet finger. Brush with egg wash or spray with cooking spray.

j. Sprinkle more cheese on top.

k. Bake for 20-25 minutes until they're golden brown and feel hollow when picked up.

l. Turn off the oven, crack the door open, and let them dry for 30 minutes.

Special Notes:

- Add a tiny pinch of cayenne pepper to the dough for a subtle kick that brings out the cheese flavor even more.
- Replace 1/4 cup of the water with white wine for extra flavor depth. The alcohol cooks off, but the taste stays!

5. Smoked Salmon Canapés

These tiny rye bread squares topped with cream cheese and smoked salmon are perfect party food. They came from Sweden and became really popular in the US during the 1950s. The mix of smoky fish, creamy cheese, and crunchy toast is so good, you'll want to make them for every get-together.

Preparation Time: 15 minutes

Cooking Time: 5 minutes

Serving Size: 16 pieces (4 servings)

Ingredients:

- 4 oz smoked salmon
- 4 oz cream cheese, softened
- 2-3 slices rye bread
- 3 tablespoons minced red onion
- 1 tablespoon fresh dill (chopped), plus extra sprigs for garnish
- 2-3 teaspoons lemon juice
- Salt and pepper to taste

Instructions:

a. Heat your oven to 450°F. You can use a regular toaster if you prefer.
b. Take your rye bread and cut off the crusts. Then cut it into small 1&1/2-inch squares. You'll need 16 squares total.
c. Put the bread squares on a baking sheet and toast them in the oven. Give them about 2-3 minutes on each side until they're nice and crispy.
d. Chop up your red onion and fresh dill.
e. Take your soft cream cheese and put it in a bowl. Use a fork to mash it until it's smooth.
f. Mix 2 tablespoons of the chopped onion and all the chopped dill into the cream cheese. Add 2 teaspoons of lemon juice, salt, and pepper. Mix everything well with your fork.
g. Taste it and add more lemon juice, dill, salt or pepper if you want.
h. Spread the cream cheese mix on each toast square.
i. Take small pieces of salmon and roll them up like little roses. Put one on top of each toast.
j. Sprinkle the leftover chopped onion on top and add a tiny sprig of dill to each one.
k. Serve right away, or you can cover them and keep them in the fridge for 1-2 hours.

Special Notes:

- Try adding a tiny dot of honey on top of each salmon rose - the sweetness works really well with the salty fish.
- You can make these even fancier by adding a few capers or a small slice of cucumber under the salmon. Some people like to add a drop of wasabi in the cream cheese mix for an extra kick.

6. Pâté en Croûte

This classic French meat pie is like a well-dressed meatloaf in a buttery crust. Born in French kitchens centuries ago, it's now a go-to dish for special occasions. The mix of pork, chicken, and liver makes it rich and tasty. It's perfect for sharing and tastes even better after waiting a couple of days.

Preparation Time: 15 minutes

Cooking Time: 3 hours

Serving Size: 20 slices

Ingredients:

For Day 1: Meat Mixture

- 2 pounds pork chop (boneless), cubed
- 1 pound fatty pork neck
- 4 tablespoons cognac
- 4 tablespoons port wine
- 12 oz chicken breast
- 1 oz salt
- 1/3 oz sugar
- 2 oz black pepper

Liver Mixture

- 8 oz chicken livers
- 3 tablespoons lemon juice
- 1 pinch sugar
- 1 teaspoon salt
- Black pepper to taste

Additional Items

- 2 egg yolks
- 2 tablespoons pistachios
- 2 cups instant Madeira gelée
- 1 recipe easy pie crust
- 2 shallots
- 2 tablespoons parsley

Instructions:

a. Day 1: Cut pork and chicken into small cubes. Mix with salt, sugar, pepper, cognac, and port wine. Put it in the fridge.
b. Cut chicken livers in half. Mix with salt, lemon juice, sugar, and pepper. Store in the fridge.
c. Day 2: Chop shallots and parsley. Cook livers in oil and butter on high heat (2-3 minutes). Add shallots and parsley, cook for 1 more minute. Set aside.
d. Roll pie dough into a big rectangle. Line your mold with it. Cut two squares for the ends and a rectangle for the top.
e. Layer the mold: First half of meat mixture, then liver mixture, then remaining meat. Press down each layer. Cover with the top dough. Make 3 holes on top. Brush with egg yolks.
f. Chill 2 hours. Heat oven to 450°F. Bake 30 minutes, then lower to 325°F for 20 more minutes.
g. Cool 4 hours. Pour gelée through the holes. Keep in the fridge 48 hours before serving.

Special Notes:

- Soak the meat in white wine instead of port for a lighter taste. Some folks like to add chopped mushrooms between the layers for an earthy touch.
- Line your mold with plastic wrap before adding the dough. It makes removing the finished loaf much easier.

7. Coquilles Saint-Jacques

This French dish from Normandy has been a hit since the 1950s. It's basically scallops swimming in a creamy sauce, topped with cheese and mashed potatoes. You'll love how the tender scallops mix with the golden-brown cheese crust. It's rich but not heavy, and perfect for date nights or fancy dinners.

Preparation Time: 25 minutes

Cooking Time: 30 minutes

Serving Size: 4 servings

Ingredients:

Mashed Potatoes:

- 2 cups russet potatoes, peeled and cubed
- 2 tablespoons heavy cream
- 2 tablespoons butter

Scallop Filling:

- 2 shallots, finely chopped
- 11 oz medium scallops (size 15-25), patted dry
- 1 cup Gruyère cheese, grated
- 2 tablespoons butter
- 2 tablespoons all-purpose flour
- 1/2 cup whole milk
- 1/4 cup white wine

Instructions:

First, make the mashed potatoes:

a. Boil the potatoes in salted water until soft
b. Drain them well
c. Mash them with butter
d. Mix in the cream until smooth and creamy
e. Put the mashed potatoes in a piping bag with a star tip

Get your oven ready:

a. Set the rack in the middle
b. Heat it to 350°F

Now for the creamy scallop sauce:

a. Cook shallots in butter until soft
b. Stir in flour and cook for 1 minute
c. Pour in milk and wine while stirring
d. Keep stirring until it bubbles
e. Cook 1 more minute
f. Take it off the heat
g. Add salt and pepper
h. Mix in scallops and half the cheese

Put it all together:

a. Split the scallop mix between 4 shells or small dishes
b. Pipe potato swirls around the edges
c. Sprinkle the rest of the cheese on top
d. Bake 10 minutes
e. Turn on the broiler for a golden-brown finish

Special Notes:

- Pat those scallops super dry with paper towels. Wet scallops will make your sauce too runny.
- Want to make it extra special? Add a tiny splash of cognac with the wine. It's not traditional, but it adds amazing flavor.

8. Ratatouille Tartlets

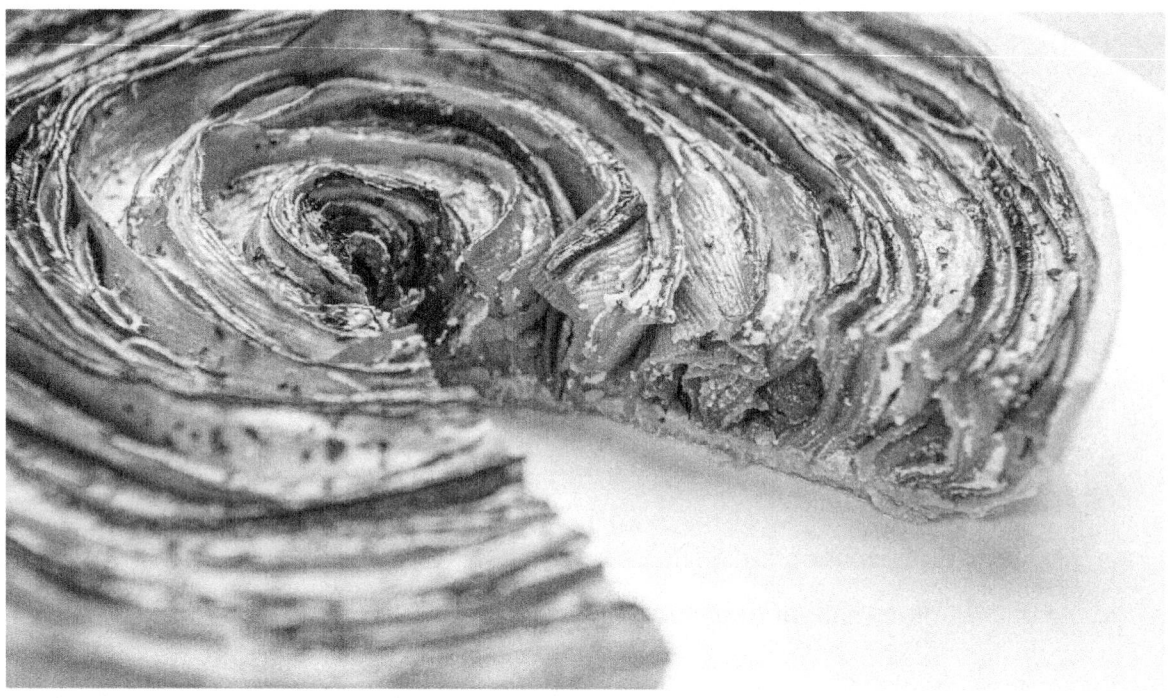

These small savory tarts come from the south of France. They're packed with summer vegetables like eggplant, zucchini, and tomatoes. People love them at parties and picnics. The cheese in the crust makes them extra tasty, and they're perfect for both hot and cold days.

Preparation Time: 40 minutes

Cooking Time: 1 hour 30 minutes

Serving Size: 8-10 servings

Ingredients:

For the pastry:

- 2&1/2 cups all-purpose flour, plus extra for dusting
- 1 egg yolk, beaten
- 1&1/3 cups (10.5 oz) unsalted butter, frozen
- 1/4 cup polenta
- 2 oz extra sharp cheddar cheese, coarsely grated
- 2 tablespoons fresh thyme leaves
- 1/2 cup very cold water

For the filling:

- 4-5 medium tomatoes (mixed colors)
- 4 garlic cloves, crushed
- 1 tablespoon sugar
- 2 medium zucchini (1 green, 1 yellow)
- 3/4 oz parmesan cheese
- 1 medium eggplant
- 2 tablespoons olive oil
- 2 medium red onions, sliced

Instructions:

The night before: Wrap butter in foil and put it in the freezer.

For the pastry:

   a. Mix flour, polenta, grated cheddar, and thyme in a big bowl
   b. Grate the frozen butter into the bowl, stirring with a knife as you go
   c. Pour in cold water and mix quickly with your hands
   d. Wrap in paper and chill for 30 minutes

For the filling:

   a. Cut all vegetables into small, even pieces
   b. Cook onions and garlic in olive oil until soft
   c. Add sugar and other vegetables
   d. Cook until tender but not mushy

Put it all together:

   a. Roll out pastry and cut into small circles
   b. Fill with vegetable mixture
   c. Top with parmesan
   d. Bake until golden

Special Notes:

- Sprinkle a tiny bit of dried lavender into the veggie mix. It adds a subtle French countryside flavor that people won't expect.
- For extra crunch, try sprinkling some toasted pine nuts on top just before serving. They're not traditional but work really well with these flavors.

9. Foie Gras on Brioche

This fancy French toast brings together buttery brioche bread and rich foie gras - a classic mix from high-end French restaurants. People go nuts for this combo at fancy brunches. It's sweet, savory, and super filling. The caramelized orange on top adds a nice bright pop.

Preparation Time: 10 minutes

Cooking Time: 20 minutes

Serving Size: 6 servings

Ingredients:

- 6 slices foie gras (about 2 oz each)
- 6 slices brioche bread
- 3 tablespoons light brown sugar
- 1 large orange
- Salt to taste
- Black pepper to taste

For Garnish:

- 1 tablespoon Madeira wine
- 2 cups mâche salad leaves

Instructions:

a. Cut the brioche into rectangles (about 1 inch × 0.8 inch) and slice them about 0.2 inch thick. Pop them in the toaster and keep them warm.
b. Cut the foie gras into 0.4-inch thick slices. Sprinkle both sides with salt and pepper.
c. Get a pan super hot. Drop in the foie gras and quickly sear each side until golden brown. Move them to an oven-safe dish.
d. Peel the orange and cut it into 0.2-inch thick round slices. Trim these into smaller circles (about 0.6 inch across). Put them on a heat-safe tray and sprinkle brown sugar on top. Use a kitchen torch to melt the sugar until it's golden and bubbly.
e. Heat your oven to 320°F. Warm up the foie gras for a few minutes.
f. Put it all together: Stack the warm foie gras on the brioche, top with the sugary orange, add some mâche leaves, and finish with a splash of Madeira.

Special Notes:

- Try storing your foie gras in the freezer for about 30 minutes before slicing - it makes getting clean, even cuts much easier.
- If you can't find mâche leaves, baby arugula works great too. The peppery kick pairs really well with the rich foie gras. Some people even like adding a tiny pinch of flaky sea salt right at the end.

10. Cheese and Charcuterie Board

This snack board comes from European traditions but has become a hit at American parties. It's basically a fancy plate of cheese, meat, and snacks that looks impressive but needs zero cooking. Perfect for when friends come over or for fancy TV watching nights.

Preparation Time: 1 hour

Cooking Time: 1 hour (for toasting bread)

Serving size: 12 people

Ingredients:

Cheeses:

- 12 oz marinated fresh mozzarella balls
- 8 oz Vermont white cheddar, cut into cubes
- 6 oz manchego cheese, thinly sliced
- 8 oz brie cheese
- 8 oz triple cream cheese (Bourgogne)

Meats:

- 8 oz salami
- 2 oz dried coppa
- 2 oz prosciutto

Pickled Stuff:

- 1 cup baby dill pickles (or gherkins)
- 1/3 cup pitted green olives
- 1/3 cup pitted kalamata olives

Fresh Fruit:

- 1 cup blueberries
- 1 apple or pear
- 2 cups grape bunches, separated
- 2 cups strawberries or figs

Spreads:

- 1/4 cup fruit spread (fig or strawberry work best)
- 1/4 cup honey

Extra Goodies:

- 1 cup mixed nuts (pecans, walnuts, or pistachios)
- 3 oz dark chocolate bar, broken up

Crackers and Bread:

- 4 oz fancy crackers
- 4 oz water crackers
- 1 baguette, sliced and toasted

Instructions:

a. Start with cheese placement - spread them around your board. Cut the hard cheeses into easy-to-grab pieces. Make the brie more inviting by cutting a few small wedges out.

b. Add your meat next. Fold the slices into fun shapes to make them look nice. You can roll them up, fold them in half, or make little roses. Put down your bowls of olives and pickles. These need their own little spaces so the juice doesn't run everywhere. Add your honey and fruit spread in small bowls. Put them next to cheeses they taste good with - like honey near the brie. Add fresh fruit around the board. Make sure everything is washed and cut into bite-sized pieces. Fill in empty spots with nuts and chocolate pieces.

c. Either arrange crackers in the remaining spaces or put them in a separate bowl nearby.

d. For the baguette slices: brush with olive oil and toast at 400°F for 6-8 minutes until golden.

Special Notes:

- Let your cheeses sit out for 30 minutes before serving - they taste way better at room temperature.
- Try adding dried apricots or dates - they're not in the recipe but they're amazing with both the cheese and meat. Plus, they fill empty spaces on the board perfectly.

Main Courses

11. Boeuf Bourguignon

This famous French beef stew comes from Burgundy region in France. The meat cooks slowly in red wine until it falls apart at the touch of your fork. The bacon adds a smoky taste while mushrooms and carrots make it hearty. It's perfect for cold days and tastes even better the next day.

Preparation Time: 40 minutes

Cooking Time: 2 hours 30 minutes

Serving Size: 8 servings

Ingredients:

- 3 lbs. beef chuck roast or stewing beef, cut into cubes
- 8 oz bacon, chopped
- 3 tbsp all-purpose flour
- 4 cups beef broth or stock, hot
- 2 cups red wine
- 12 oz mushrooms, cut in half
- 1/2 tsp black pepper
- 1 large onion, chopped
- 2 medium carrots, chopped
- 1 lb. baby potatoes, cut in half (optional)
- 3 tbsp tomato paste
- 3 cloves garlic, minced
- 2 sprigs fresh thyme (or 1/2 tsp dried thyme)
- 1 sprig fresh rosemary (or 1/2 tsp dried rosemary)
- 1 tsp salt
- 1 bay leaf
- Fresh parsley for topping

Instructions:

a. Turn your oven on to 325°F.
b. Get a big pot that can go in the oven. Cook the bacon until crispy. Take it out but leave the fat in the pot.
c. Pat the beef dry with paper towels. Put salt and pepper on it. Cook the meat in small batches until brown on all sides. Put the cooked meat on a plate.
d. Put onions and carrots in the same pot. Cook them for 2-3 minutes until onions look see-through.
e. Put the meat back in. Sprinkle flour over everything and stir for 2-3 minutes.
f. Pour in hot broth and wine. Add mushrooms, potatoes (if using), tomato paste, garlic, thyme, rosemary, and bay leaf.
g. Put the lid on and let it cook in the oven for 2 1/2 to 3 hours.
h. Take out the bay leaf. Mix in most of the bacon, but save some for topping. Taste it and add more salt and pepper if needed.

Special Notes:

- Use a Pinot Noir wine if you can - it's from the same region as this dish and makes the sauce taste amazing. Don't use expensive wine though, any decent red wine works fine.
- Try adding 1-2 tablespoons of butter mixed with flour (called beurre manié) at the end if you want the sauce thicker. Just drop small bits in while stirring until you're happy with how thick it is.

12. Coq au Vin

This classic French dish has been around since the 16th century. It's basically chicken cooked in wine until it's super tender. The French make it with red wine and bacon, which gives it a rich taste that's hard to beat. Perfect for cold nights or when you want to feel fancy without too much work.

Preparation Time: 25 minutes

Cooking Time: 2 hours 30 minutes (plus marinating)

Serving Size: 6

Ingredients:

- 4 pounds chicken thighs (about 4 thighs)
- 6 pounds boneless chicken breasts (about 2 breasts)
- 12 whole shallots, peeled
- 1 pound chicken legs (about 2 legs)
- 3 garlic cloves, finely chopped
- 3 tablespoons brandy or Cognac
- 5 cups red wine
- 2/3 cup chicken stock
- 1 tablespoon olive oil, plus extra for mushrooms
- 3 ounces dry-cured smoked bacon, chopped
- 2 teaspoons tomato paste
- 3 sprigs thyme
- 2 sprigs rosemary
- 2 bay leaves
- Fresh parsley for garnish

For the mushrooms:

- 8 ounces chestnut mushrooms
- 1 tablespoon olive oil

For the thickener:

- 1 teaspoon soft butter
- 2 tablespoons all-purpose flour
- 1 teaspoon olive oil

Instructions:

a. Get your biggest pot hot and add oil. Cook the chopped bacon until crispy. Take it out and save it for later.
b. Put the shallots in the same pot. Cook them for about 8 minutes until they're brown all over. Take them out too.
c. Remove all chicken skin. Cook the chicken pieces in two batches until they're golden brown (about 8 minutes each batch).
d. Throw in the garlic, cook for a minute. Pour in the brandy and scrape all the good stuff off the bottom of the pot.
e. Put the chicken legs and thighs back in. Add wine gradually, then stock and tomato paste.
f. Tie up the herbs (thyme, rosemary, bay leaves) and drop them in. Add the bacon and shallots back. Season with salt and pepper.
g. Cover and let it simmer. After 10 minutes, add the chicken breasts. Cook everything for about an hour.
h. When you're almost ready to eat, cook the mushrooms in oil until golden.
i. Take out all the chicken and vegetables. Mix the flour, oil, and butter to make a paste.
j. Get the sauce bubbling and whisk in small bits of the paste until it thickens.
k. Put everything back together: chicken first, then mushrooms, pour the sauce over, and top with parsley.

Special Notes:

- Marinade the chicken overnight in half the wine with some crushed black peppercorns. This makes the meat even more tender and flavorful.
- If you don't have brandy, use a splash of bourbon or even some white wine vinegar mixed with a teaspoon of honey. It gives a similar sweet-tangy kick that the recipe needs.

13. Duck Confit (Confit de Canard)

This old French recipe turns tough duck legs into something amazing - so tender the meat falls off the bone. People in France have been making it for hundreds of years. It's not quick, but it's worth the wait. The meat gets super soft by cooking it very slowly in duck fat.

Preparation Time: 15 minutes

Cooking Time: 8 hours 50 minutes

Serving Size: 4 servings

Ingredients:

For the Duck:

- 4 duck legs (8 oz each), with skin and bone
- 3&1/4 cups duck fat

For the Seasoning Mix:

- 4 teaspoons kosher salt
- 1/3 cup fresh thyme sprigs
- 8 star anise
- 2 bay leaves
- 2 tablespoons juniper berries
- 8 whole cloves
- 1/3 cup fresh sage sprigs
- 1/3 cup fresh rosemary sprigs
- 1/3 cup fresh oregano sprigs
- 6 garlic cloves, smashed with skin on
- 1 shallot, sliced 1/3-inch thick
- 1 tablespoon black peppercorns
- 1 tablespoon coriander seeds

Instructions:

a. Mix the duck legs with all the seasoning ingredients in a big bowl. Put everything in a glass or ceramic dish where the legs fit in one layer. Cover and leave in the fridge for 12-24 hours.
b. Take the legs out and wash off all the seasoning under running water. Dry them well with paper towels.
c. Heat your oven to 210°F.
d. Put the duck legs in a small metal pan with high sides. They should touch each other but stay in one layer.
e. Pour the duck fat over the legs until they're covered.
f. Put the pan on the stove and heat until the fat bubbles all over.
g. Cut a piece of baking paper to fit the pan. Place it right on top of the fat. Cover the pan tightly with two layers of foil.
h. Cook in the oven for 8 hours.
i. Check if it's done by taking out one leg - the meat should be super soft.
j. To make the skin crispy:

- Heat oven to 465°F
- Put the legs on a rack over a pan with 1 inch of hot water
- Cook for 40 minutes until the skin turns golden and crispy

Special Notes:

- Add orange zest to the seasoning mix. The citrus oils make the meat taste even better.
- Try this: Instead of using all duck fat, you can use half duck fat and half good olive oil. Some French home cooks do this, and it works great.

14. Bouillabaisse

This famous seafood stew comes from Marseille, France. It started as a simple fishermen's meal but became super popular worldwide. You'll get all kinds of seafood swimming in a rich broth with fresh herbs. It's like having the ocean in your bowl, but way tastier!

Preparation Time: 20 minutes

Cooking Time: 25 minutes

Serving Size: 4 people

Ingredients:

- 1 pound halibut, cut into 2-inch pieces
- 1 pound mixed clams and/or mussels, cleaned
- 8 ounces scallops (about 6-8 pieces)
- 8 ounces medium shrimp
- 2 tablespoons olive oil
- 2 large tomatoes, chopped
- 3-4 sprigs fresh thyme
- 1 pinch saffron
- 1 large orange peel
- 1 bay leaf
- 2 tablespoons unsalted butter
- 1 leek, thinly sliced and cleaned well
- 1 small fennel, sliced
- 4 cloves garlic, finely chopped
- 2 tablespoons tomato paste
- 4 cups seafood stock
- 1/2 teaspoon kosher salt
- 1/4 teaspoon black pepper
- Fresh parsley, chopped for topping

Instructions:

a. Get your biggest pot hot over medium heat. Drop in the oil and butter.
b. Once they're melted together, throw in your leeks and fennel. Let them cook until they're soft and smell good - about 2-3 minutes. Don't let them turn brown!
c. Add garlic and cook for a minute. Stir in tomato paste and cook another 30 seconds.
d. Toss in your chopped tomatoes. Add saffron and cook everything for 3-4 minutes until the tomatoes start getting soft.
e. Pour in the seafood stock. Add thyme, bay leaf, and orange peel. Let it bubble away for 15-20 minutes.
f. Now comes the fun part - adding the seafood in order:
   - First goes the halibut - cook 3-4 minutes
   - Next, add clams and mussels - cook 3-4 minutes
   - Then scallops - cook 2-3 minutes
   - Finally, add shrimp - cook 2-3 minutes
g. When the shrimp turn pink and the shellfish open up, you're done! Give the broth a taste and add salt if needed.

1. Fill up your bowls with plenty of seafood and broth. Sprinkle fresh parsley on top.

Special Notes:

- Drop a piece of orange rind with some of the white pith still attached - it adds a subtle bitterness that makes the broth even better.
- Make it extra fancy: Rub a piece of crusty bread with garlic, toast it, and float it on top of your bowl. The French call this a "rouille" and it soaks up the amazing broth!

15. Cassoulet

This hearty French dish comes from the countryside where people love slow-cooked meals. It mixes tender white beans with rich duck meat and sausages. The locals say this meal is best shared with friends and family on cold days. Some call it France's answer to baked beans, but way fancier!

Preparation Time: 15 minutes (plus 24 hours soaking)

Cooking Time: 3 hours 45 minutes

Serving Size: 4 people

Ingredients:

- 1 pound Tarbais beans (or great northern beans)
- 4 duck and Armagnac sausages
- 1 French garlic sausage
- 4 garlic cloves, smashed
- 1 small onion, cut in half
- 3 whole cloves
- 1 medium carrot, roughly chopped
- 4 ounces salt pork (ventrèche)
- 4 tablespoons duck fat, room temperature
- 3 duck leg confit pieces
- 8 ounces duck and veal demi-glace
- 1 tablespoon tomato paste
- Salt and black pepper to taste
- For bouquet garni:
    - 5 parsley sprigs
    - 1 thyme sprig
    - 1 bay leaf
    - 10 peppercorns

Instructions:

a. Soak beans overnight (24 hours) in a big bowl with lots of water.
b. Next day, drain beans and put them in a pot. Add half the salt pork, garlic, carrot, the tied-up herbs (bouquet garni), and onion. Cover with water and cook for 1 hour until the beans are just soft.
c. While beans cook:

- Brown the duck sausages in a pan
- Cut sausages into chunks
- Slice garlic sausage
- Split duck legs at joints

d. Heat oven to 325°F.
e. When beans are done:

- Take out herbs and onion
- Cut cooked salt pork into small cubes
- Mix demi-glace sauce with water and tomato paste

f. Layer everything in a big pot:

- Grease pot with duck fat
- Add half the beans
- Put in all meats
- Add more duck fat
- Top with remaining beans
- Pour sauce over everything
- Finish with duck fat on top

g. Bake for 2 1/2-3 hours uncovered. Check and add water if it is too dry.

h. Turn up the heat to 400°F and cook for 45 more minutes until the top is brown and crusty.

Special Notes:

- Add a splash of white wine to the bean cooking water - it helps break down the beans faster and adds extra flavor.
- No Tarbais beans? Great northern beans or navy beans work fine. Just make sure to get dried beans, not canned ones - they hold up better during the long cooking time.

16. Steak au Poivre

This famous French steak dish has been around since the 19th century. The mix of crushed peppercorns gives the meat an amazing kick, while the cream sauce adds a smooth, rich touch. It's the kind of steak that makes you feel like you're eating at a fancy restaurant in Paris.

Preparation Time: 15 minutes

Cooking Time: 20-25 minutes

Serving Size: 4 people

Ingredients:

- 4 beef tenderloin steaks (6 oz each)
- 1/4 cup Cognac or brandy
- 1/2 cup beef stock
- 1/2 cup heavy cream
- 1 small shallot
- 2 tablespoons mixed peppercorns (black, white, pink, and red)
- 1 teaspoon kosher salt
- 1 tablespoon olive oil
- 3 tablespoons unsalted butter

Instructions:

a. Take the steaks out of the fridge. Remove any twine and let them sit for 30 minutes to warm up.
b. While waiting, chop up the shallot into tiny pieces.
c. Put the peppercorns in a clean kitchen towel and smash them with something heavy (like a pan) until they're broken but not powdered.
d. Sprinkle salt all over the steaks. Press the crushed peppercorns onto both sides of each steak with your hands.
e. Get a big skillet super hot (until you see smoke). Add oil and 1 tablespoon butter.
f. Cook the steaks for about 2-3 minutes on each side for medium-rare (130°F inside). Put them on a plate and cover with foil.
g. Turn down the heat to medium. Add another tablespoon of butter and cook the shallots for 1 minute.
h. Take the pan off the heat, pour in the Cognac, then put it back on medium heat. Scrape all the tasty bits off the bottom until most of the liquid is gone.
i. Pour in the beef stock and turn up the heat. Let it bubble for 2-3 minutes.
j. Add cream and the last tablespoon of butter. Keep stirring until it gets thick enough to coat a spoon.
k. Pour in any juice from the steak plate. Put the steaks on plates and cover them with sauce.

Special Notes:

- Try crushing the peppercorns with a wine bottle if you don't have a heavy pan. The round shape makes it easier to roll and crush.
- For extra flavor, drop a small pat of herb butter (not in the ingredient list) on top of each steak right before serving. It will melt into the hot pepper crust and make everything even better.

17. Sole Meunière

This classic French dish has been around since forever in fancy restaurants. It's just fish cooked in butter with lemon - super simple but tastes amazing. Julia Child fell in love with it when she first tried it in France. If you like fish that's crispy outside but tender inside, you'll want to make this.

Preparation Time: 10 minutes

Cooking Time: 15 minutes

Serving Size: 2 people

Ingredients:

- 1/2 cup all-purpose flour
- 4 pieces sole fillets (3-4 oz each), patted dry
- 2 tablespoons vegetable oil
- 2 tablespoons fresh parsley, finely chopped
- 6 tablespoons unsalted butter, split use
- 1 tablespoon fresh lemon juice
- Salt and black pepper to taste
- Lemon wedges for serving

Instructions:

a. Put the flour in a shallow dish.
b. Pat the fish dry with paper towels. Sprinkle both sides with salt and pepper.
c. Coat each fillet in flour. Shake off any extra flour and put them on a plate.
d. Put a large pan on medium-high heat. Add 2 tablespoons butter and the oil.
e. When the butter starts bubbling, add the fish. Cook until it's golden brown on the bottom (about 2 minutes).
f. Carefully flip the fish with a spatula. Cook another minute until it's done.
g. Move the fish to warm plates and cover with foil to keep warm.
h. Clean out the pan with a paper towel.
i. Add the rest of the butter (4 tablespoons) to the pan. Let it cook until it turns golden and smells nutty (about 2 minutes).
j. Take the pan off the heat. Add the parsley and lemon juice right away. Watch out - the butter might splash!
k. Pour the butter sauce over the fish. Put lemon wedges on the side.

Special Notes:

- Try sprinkling a tiny bit of cayenne pepper in the flour - it adds a nice kick without making it spicy.
- If you can't find a sole, any thin white fish like flounder or tilapia works great too. Just make sure it's fresh and not too thick, or it won't cook right.

18. Herb-Crusted Lamb Rack (Carré d'Agneau)

This fancy lamb dish comes from French cooking tradition. It's a top choice in high-end restaurants but you can make it at home too. The crispy herb coating makes the juicy lamb taste even better. If you want to impress someone with your cooking skills, this recipe will do the job.

Preparation Time: 10 minutes

Cooking Time: 20 minutes

Serving Size: 4 people

Ingredients:

Lamb

- 2 large racks of lamb (about 8 chops each), at room temp
- 5 tablespoons olive oil
- Sea salt, to taste
- Black pepper, to taste

Herb Crust

- 1 cup Panko breadcrumbs
- 2 large garlic cloves, crushed
- 1 tablespoon olive oil
- 1/4 cup Dijon mustard
- 1/4 cup chopped parsley
- 1/4 cup grated Parmesan cheese
- 1 tablespoon Herbes de Provence

Instructions:

a. Turn your oven on to 425°F
b. Get your lamb ready:

- Pat the meat dry
- Sprinkle salt and pepper all over, even the ends

c. Cook the lamb:

- Heat oil in a cast iron pan
- Brown the lamb on all sides
- Put the pan in the oven for 8 minutes with the fatty side down

d. While waiting, mix your crust:

- Put breadcrumbs, parsley, cheese, herbs, garlic and oil in a blender
- Blend until everything sticks together

e. Finish it up:

- Take the lamb out
- Brush mustard all over it
- Press the herb mix onto the mustard
- Put it back in the oven for 4 minutes
- Let it rest for 10-15 minutes before cutting

Special Notes:

- Rub a cut garlic clove on the hot pan before cooking the lamb. This adds an extra layer of flavor without being too strong.
- Add 2 tablespoons of finely chopped fresh mint to the crust mixture. Mint and lamb are best friends in cooking.

19. Ratatouille

This famous French dish comes from Nice. It's basically a bunch of fresh veggies cooked together until they're super soft and tasty. People love it hot or cold, and it's perfect when you want something light but filling. The slow cooking makes all the veggies blend their flavors together really well.

Preparation Time: 20 minutes

Cooking Time: 1 hour 10 minutes

Serving Size: 6 servings

Ingredients:

- 4 tablespoons olive oil (split in half)
- 1/3 cup carrot, shredded
- 1 can (14 oz) crushed tomatoes
- 2 teaspoons dried basil
- 4 garlic cloves, minced
- 1 small eggplant, cut into 1/8-inch circles
- 2 small zucchini, cut into 1/8-inch circles
- 3 Roma tomatoes, cut into 1/8-inch circles
- 1/2 cup onion, chopped
- 1/2 teaspoon dried parsley
- Salt to taste
- Black pepper to taste

Instructions:

a. Turn your oven on to 375°F. Get a big non-stick pan and heat up half the olive oil.
b. Throw in your chopped onion, minced garlic, and shredded carrot.
c. Cook them until they're soft - about 5 minutes.
d. Pour in the crushed tomatoes and add the basil and parsley. Let it bubble away for 15 minutes until it gets thick. Give it a taste and add salt and pepper if needed.
e. Get a 2-quart baking dish and pour in your tomato sauce. Now comes the fun part - stand your veggie slices up in circles, mixing the eggplant, zucchini, and tomatoes. Think of it like making a veggie domino circle! Brush the rest of the olive oil over the top.
f. Cover the dish with foil and pop it in the oven for 30 minutes. Then take the foil off and keep cooking until you can easily stick a fork through the veggies.
g. Serve it right away while it's hot and steamy.

Special Notes:

- Before you start, salt your eggplant slices and let them sit for 15 minutes. This pulls out extra water and any bitterness. Just pat them dry before using.
- Try adding a sprinkle of herbes de Provence instead of just basil and parsley. It's what French grandmas use, and it makes everything taste amazing!

20. Salmon en Croûte (Saumon en Croûte)

This French-style wrapped salmon is a hit at dinner parties. It's basically a fancy fish sandwich - tender salmon and creamy spinach wrapped in flaky pastry. The French made it fancy, but really it's just good comfort food that looks amazing when you serve it.

Preparation Time: 15 minutes

Cooking Time: 40 minutes

Serving Size: 6-8 people

Ingredients:

- 1 pound salmon fillet (about 1 inch thick)
- 1 sheet puff pastry (15 × 10 inches), room temperature
- 5 ounces baby spinach
- 4 ounces cream cheese
- 1/2 cup grated Parmesan cheese
- 1 teaspoon dried dill
- 3/4 cup panko bread crumbs
- 1 large egg, beaten
- 2 tablespoons olive oil
- 1 medium yellow onion, finely chopped
- 2 cloves garlic, finely chopped
- Salt and black pepper to taste

Instructions:

a. Start your oven - set it to 400°F. Salt your salmon well and pop it in the fridge for 15 minutes.
b. While waiting, cook the filling:

- Heat oil in a big pan
- Cook onion and garlic with some salt until see-through (about 5 minutes)
- Throw in spinach and stir until it starts getting soft
- Mix in cream cheese, Parmesan, and dill until melted
- Add 1/2 cup panko and stir until thick
- Add salt and pepper how you like it

c. Get your salmon ready:

- Rinse off the salt
- Dry it with paper towels
- Put it in the middle of your puff pastry sheet
- Cover the top with your spinach mix
- Sprinkle the last 1/4 cup panko on top

d. Wrap it up:

- Fold the long sides over the salmon
- Fold up the short ends
- Flip it over onto a baking sheet with parchment
- Brush egg all over
- Cut some diagonal lines on top

e. Bake for 25-35 minutes until golden brown and salmon reads 140°F inside. Let it rest a few minutes, then slice and serve.

Special Notes:

- Try spreading a thin layer of Dijon mustard on the salmon before adding the spinach mix - it adds a nice kick.
- Let your puff pastry get soft at room temperature for 40 minutes instead of just 30. It'll be easier to work with and puff up better in the oven.

Sweets

21. Classic Crème Brûlée

This smooth French dessert has been around since the 1700s. You'll get a silky vanilla custard hidden under a layer of crispy caramel that breaks like thin ice when you tap it with your spoon. It looks fancy but needs just 5 ingredients. Perfect for dinner parties or date nights.

Preparation Time: 20 minutes

Cooking Time: 40 minutes

Serving Size: 6 servings

Ingredients: For the Custard:

- 2 cups heavy whipping cream
- 1/2 cup sugar
- 5 large egg yolks
- 1 teaspoon vanilla extract (or vanilla bean paste)
- 1 pinch fine sea salt

For the Top:

- 9-12 teaspoons sugar (1 1/2 to 2 teaspoons per ramekin)

Instructions:

a. Set your oven to 300°F. Heat the cream in a pot over medium heat. Stir it now and then until you see steam rising. Add vanilla, then take it off the heat.
b. Mix egg yolks, sugar, and salt in a bowl. Here's the tricky part - pour the hot cream into the egg mix very slowly while stirring. If you rush this, you'll end up with scrambled eggs!
c. Pour everything through a strainer into a container you can easily pour from. Throw away whatever stays in the strainer.
d. Fill six 4-ounce ramekins with the mixture. Put them in a 9x13 baking pan.
e. Pour boiling water into the pan, filling it halfway up the ramekins' edges.
f. Bake for 30-35 minutes. They're done when they still have a tiny wobble in the middle. Let them cool on a rack, then put them in the fridge for at least 2 hours.
g. When you're ready to serve, sprinkle sugar evenly on top of each custard. Use a torch to melt the sugar, moving in circles until it turns amber brown.

Special Notes:

- Want extra flavor? Split a vanilla bean and scrape the seeds into the cream instead of using extract. The tiny black specs look pretty and taste amazing.
- If you don't have a torch, put the sugared tops under your oven's broiler for 2-3 minutes. Watch them like a hawk - they can burn fast!

22. Chocolate Soufflé

This French chocolate dessert makes everyone go "wow!" You'll get a soft, airy chocolate treat that puffs up like magic in the oven. It's been around since the 1800s in Paris, and there's a good reason why fancy restaurants still serve it today. The crispy top and gooey middle will make you fall in love.

Preparation Time: 30 minutes

Cooking Time: 14 minutes

Serving Size: 4 servings (6-ounce soufflés)

Ingredients: For the Soufflé Batter:

- 4 oz semi-sweet chocolate bar, chopped
- 3 large eggs, separated
- 1 teaspoon vanilla extract
- 1/4 cup unsalted butter, cut into 4 pieces
- 3 tablespoons sugar
- 1/8 teaspoon salt
- 1/8 teaspoon cream of tartar

For the Ramekins:

- 4 teaspoons sugar
- 1 tablespoon soft unsalted butter

Instructions:

a. Melt butter and chocolate together. You can use a double boiler or microwave in 20-second bursts, stirring each time. Let it cool for 5 minutes.
b. Mix in egg yolks, vanilla, and salt with the chocolate. Set aside.
c. In a super clean bowl, beat egg whites and cream of tartar until they form soft peaks. Slowly add sugar, one tablespoon at a time.
d. Continue pounding until the peaks are stiff and lustrous.
e. Fold egg whites into chocolate mix in three parts.
f. Be gentle; you want to keep all of the air in!
g. Pop the mix in the fridge for 5-10 minutes while you get everything else ready.
h. Heat oven to 400°F. Put the rack in the lower third.
i. Butter four 6-ounce ramekins really well. Coat with sugar, making sure to cover all sides.
j. Fill ramekins with the mix. Smooth the tops and run your finger around the edge to make a little groove.
k. Put them in the oven and quickly turn the heat down to 375°F.
l. Bake for 13-14 minutes until the edges are set but the middle still jiggles a bit.
m. Serve right away - these guys start sinking after a few minutes!

Special Notes:

- Want to make it extra special? Add 1/4 teaspoon of espresso powder to the chocolate mixture. Coffee makes chocolate taste even more chocolatey!
- For the best rise, make sure your egg whites are at room temperature and your bowl is completely grease-free. Even a tiny bit of egg yolk or butter will stop them from whipping up properly.

23. Upside-Down Apple Pie (Tarte Tatin)

This classic French dessert was accidentally created in the 1880s at Hotel Tatin in Loire Valley. It's basically an apple pie turned on its head - sweet caramel and apples on the bottom, buttery crust on top. The apples get super soft and golden brown, making it a perfect dessert for cold nights.

Preparation Time: 30 minutes

Cooking Time: 60 minutes

Serving Size: 6-8 servings

Ingredients:

For the Crust:

- 2&1/2 cups all-purpose flour
- 10&1/2 oz soft butter
- 1 large egg
- 1/2 cup sugar
- 1 pinch salt

For the Filling:

- 8 Golden Delicious apples
- 3-4 star anise (optional)

For the Caramel:

- 7 tablespoons butter
- 3/4 cup sugar
- 2 tablespoons water

Instructions:

a. Let butter come to room temp. Mix flour, butter, sugar, beaten egg, and salt in a bowl. Use a spoon first, then your hands to make it crumbly.
b. Knead for 30 seconds into a ball, flatten it, wrap in plastic, and chill 2+ hours.
c. Cut off apple tops and bottoms. Peel them and remove cores.
d. Save the cut parts for smoothies if you want!
e. Cook the apples: Melt 1 tablespoon butter in a pan over medium heat.
f. Add apples, coat with butter, cover, and cook for 5 minutes. Let cool.
g. Make caramel: Put sugar and water in a pot with star anise. Heat until brown.
h. Add butter pieces slowly while stirring. Be super careful - hot caramel burns are no joke!
i. Pour caramel into an 8-inch cake pan with high sides.
j. Roll out cold dough on a floured surface to 1/2 inch thick. Cut into a circle slightly bigger than your pan.
k. Stand apple quarters around the pan's edge in the caramel. Put two pieces in the middle.
l. Cover with pastry, tuck edges down, poke holes with a fork.
m. Bake at 350°F for 50 minutes until the crust looks done.
n. Cool for 20 minutes, then flip onto a plate. Serve warm or room temp.

Special Notes:

- Try using Pink Lady or Honeycrisp apples instead of Golden Delicious - they hold their shape better when baked and add a nice tartness.
- Before adding the pastry, sprinkle some crushed pecans over the apples. They'll toast while baking and add a nutty crunch to every bite.

24. Macarons

These sweet, round cookies came from France in the 1500s. They look like tiny colorful hamburgers but taste like heaven. People love them because they're crunchy outside but soft inside. You can fill them with anything you want - buttercream, chocolate, or jam. They're tricky to make but worth every bite.

Preparation Time: 60 minutes

Cooking Time: 30 minutes

Serving Size: 4

Ingredients: For the Cookies:

- 7 medium egg whites, room temp (better if they're a day old)
- 1 cup granulated sugar
- 2/3 cup water
- 2 cups blanched almond flour
- 2 cups confectioners' sugar
- 1/4 teaspoon fine salt
- Food coloring paste (any color you like)

For the Buttercream Filling:

- 1/4 teaspoon fine salt
- 1 pound unsalted butter, room temp, cut into cubes
- 1 & 3/4 cups granulated sugar
- 1 cup water
- 5 medium egg whites
- 1 vanilla bean (or 2 teaspoons vanilla extract)

Instructions:

Mix the Dry Stuff

   a. Sift almond flour, sugar, and salt
   b. Mix them well in a bowl
   c. Add 3 egg whites and stir until you get a paste

Make Sugar Syrup

   a. Heat sugar and water to 238°F
   b. Don't stir it while heating

Make the Cookie Mix

   a. Beat 4 egg whites until fluffy
   b. Pour hot sugar syrup in slowly
   c. Beat until shiny and warm
   d. Add food coloring if you want
   e. Mix this with your almond paste until it flows like slow lava

Shape and Bake

   a. Pipe 1.5-inch circles on parchment paper
   b. Let them sit for 30 minutes until dry to touch
   c. Bake at 300°F for 15-20 minutes
   d. Let them cool completely

Make Buttercream

    a. Heat sugar and water to 238°F
    b. Beat egg whites with salt and sugar until fluffy
    c. Add hot syrup slowly
    d. Beat until cool
    e. Mix in butter bit by bit
    f. Add vanilla

Put Them Together

    a. Pipe buttercream on half the cookies
    b. Top with remaining cookies
    c. Freeze overnight for best taste

Special Notes:

- Age your egg whites! Leave them on the counter for 24-48 hours before using. This helps make better cookies.
- Try adding a pinch of cream of tartar to your egg whites. It helps them whip up better and makes your macarons more stable. Also, tapping the baking sheet hard on the counter 3-4 times helps get rid of air bubbles that could crack your macarons.

25. Profiteroles

These small, puffy pastries are a French classic that's now loved worldwide. They're made with simple ingredients like butter, flour, and eggs, but transform into hollow, airy shells perfect for cream filling. Top them with warm chocolate sauce and you've got something really special.

Preparation Time: 1 hour

Cooking Time: 30 minutes

Serving Size: Makes 20 puffs

Ingredients:

For the Pastry Shells:

- 1 cup plain flour
- 4 tsp sugar
- 1 cup water
- 6 oz unsalted butter
- 1 pinch salt
- 3 medium eggs, beaten

For the Cream Filling:

- 1 orange, zested
- 2&1/2 cups heavy cream

For the Chocolate Sauce:

- 7 oz dark chocolate, broken into pieces
- 1/2 cup water
- 1/3 cup sugar

Instructions:

Heat your oven to 400°F. Put a roasting pan in the bottom of the oven.

Make the pastry shells:

a. Heat water, butter, and sugar in a pot until butter melts
b. Crank up the heat and dump in all the flour and salt at once
c. Stir like crazy until you get a smooth ball of dough that pulls away from the sides
d. Let it cool in a bowl for 15 minutes
e. Mix in beaten eggs bit by bit until smooth and shiny

Shape and bake:

a. Pipe small dough balls onto a greased baking sheet
b. Pat each top with wet finger to smooth
c. Pour 1/2 cup water in the hot roasting pan
d. Bake 25-30 minutes until golden brown
e. Poke a hole in bottom of each puff
f. Return to cooling oven for 5 minutes to dry out

Make the fillings:

a. Whip cream with orange zest until soft peaks form
b. For sauce, melt chocolate over simmering sugar-water
c. Mix melted chocolate with sugar syrup until smooth

Fill cooled puffs with cream using a piping bag. Pour warm chocolate sauce over them when serving.

Special Notes:

- Add 1/4 teaspoon vanilla bean paste to the cream filling - it makes the flavor pop without changing the classic taste
- Freeze unfilled puffs for up to a month. Just crisp them in a 350°F oven for 5 minutes before filling

26. Madeleines

These small, seashell-shaped cookies from France have been a hit since the 1700s. The recipe uses basic ingredients but gives you amazing buttery, light, and spongy cookies. They're perfect with tea or coffee, and the light dusting of sugar makes them look extra fancy.

Preparation Time: 20 minutes

Chill Time: 1 hour

Cooking Time: 8 minutes

Serving size: 20 cookies

Ingredients:

- 3/4 cup plus 1 tablespoon all-purpose flour, sifted
- 7 tablespoons unsalted butter (plus extra for greasing pans)
- 2 large eggs, room temperature
- 1/4 teaspoon baking powder
- 1 pinch salt
- 1/2 cup granulated sugar
- 1 teaspoon lemon zest
- 1 teaspoon pure vanilla extract
- Powdered sugar for dusting

Instructions:

a. Melt the butter in a microwave or pot. For extra flavor, let it brown until golden. Set aside to cool.
b. Mix the dry stuff: Put flour, salt, and baking powder in a bowl. Give it a good whisk.
c. Beat eggs and sugar in a mixer with the whisk part. Go for 8-9 minutes until it's thick and pale yellow. The mix should leave trails when you lift the whisk. Add vanilla and lemon zest at the end.
d. Add the flour mix to the egg mix. Fold it in gently - don't overdo it! You can put the flour through a strainer while folding to avoid lumps.
e. Pour in the cooled butter and mix just until it's combined.
f. Put the batter in the fridge for 1 hour. Butter your madeleine pans and chill them too.
g. Heat oven to 350°F. Put 1 tablespoon of batter in each shell shape.
h. Bake for 8-10 minutes until done. Dust with powdered sugar before serving.

Special Notes:

- Get your eggs super fluffy: Leave them out for 2-3 hours before using. Cold eggs won't fluff up as nicely.
- Try orange zest instead of lemon, or add 1/4 teaspoon of almond extract with the vanilla for a nutty twist. Both work great with the buttery taste.

27. Éclairs

These cream-filled pastries are a French classic that's been around since the 1800s. They're basically airy pastry tubes filled with smooth vanilla cream and topped with dark chocolate. They're perfect for parties or when you want to treat yourself to something fancy without spending too much time in the kitchen.

Preparation Time: 60 minutes

Cooking Time: 60 minutes

Serving Size: 24 pieces

Ingredients:

For the Pastry Shells:

- 1 batch Choux Pastry (use half milk, half water, plus optional sugar)

For the Filling:

- 1 batch vanilla pastry cream
- Cooking spray

For the Chocolate Top:

- 3/4 cup dark chocolate (70% cocoa), chopped
- 1 tablespoon light corn syrup
- 4 tablespoons unsalted butter, cut small
- 1/8 teaspoon kosher salt (or 1/16 teaspoon table salt)

Instructions:

a. Heat oven to 350°F. Draw twenty-four 4 1/2-inch lines on two pieces of parchment paper, keeping them 2 inches apart. Flip papers over and put them on baking sheets.
b. Stick down paper corners with tiny bits of pastry dough.
c. Make the shells:
   - Hold piping bag at an angle
   - Pipe 1-inch wide strips along your drawn lines
   - Smooth any bumps with a wet finger
   - Spray lightly with cooking spray
d. Bake shells one tray at a time for 30 minutes until they're golden and feel hollow.
e. While still hot, poke two small holes in the bottom of each shell.
f. Let shells dry in the warm (turned-off) oven with the door cracked open for 30 minutes.
g. Fill each shell through both holes with vanilla cream.
h. Make chocolate topping:
   - Mix chocolate, butter, corn syrup, and salt
   - Microwave in 15-second bursts, stirring each time
   - Heat until smooth (about 1 minute total)
i. Dip the top of each pastry in chocolate. Let set for 30 minutes before eating.

Special Notes:

- Add a tiny pinch of instant espresso powder to the chocolate topping - it won't taste like coffee but will make the chocolate flavor pop!
- Make them mini: Use a smaller piping tip and make 2-inch lines instead of 4&1/2-inch ones for bite-sized treats. Just remember to reduce baking time by about 5-7 minutes.

28. Crêpes Suzette

Born in fancy French restaurants in the 1890s, these thin pancakes swimming in orange butter sauce are now super popular worldwide. They're basically delicate French pancakes with a kick of orange liqueur. You'll love how the warm orange sauce makes the whole thing taste amazing, especially with cold ice cream on top.

Preparation Time: 45 minutes (including 20 minutes resting time)

Cooking Time: 20 minutes

Serving Size: 6-8 servings

Ingredients:

For the Crêpes:

- 1 cup all-purpose flour
- 1/2 cup milk
- 2 teaspoons orange juice
- 1&1/2 teaspoons orange zest
- 1/4 teaspoon salt
- 7 tablespoons water
- 2 large eggs
- 2 tablespoons melted unsalted butter (plus extra for cooking)

For the Orange Sauce:

- 1/2 cup orange liqueur like Grand Marnier (divided)
- 1 cup unsalted butter (divided)
- 4 tablespoons sugar (divided)

For Serving:

- 1 pint vanilla ice cream

Instructions:

Mix your crêpe batter: Put flour, milk, water, eggs, 2 tablespoons melted butter, orange juice, zest, and salt in a bowl. Whisk until smooth. Let it chill in the fridge for 20 minutes.

Make the crêpes:

a. Heat a pan on medium-low
b. Brush with butter
c. Pour 3 tablespoons batter, tilt pan to spread
d. Cook 1 minute until golden underneath
e. Flip and cook another minute
f. Keep warm and repeat with remaining batter

Make the orange sauce:

a. Melt half the butter in a big pan
b. Take pan off heat
c. Add half the sugar
d. Pour in half the orange liqueur (it will flame up - that's okay!)
e. When flames die down, dip each crêpe in sauce
f. Fold crêpes into quarters

Make more sauce with remaining butter, sugar, and liqueur the same way.

Put 1-2 crêpes on each plate, add ice cream, pour extra sauce on top. Serve right away.

Special Notes:

- Add a tiny pinch of cardamom to the batter - it works magic with the orange flavor
- Make these extra special by adding some finely grated dark chocolate on top just before serving - the warm sauce will melt it perfectly

29. Christmas Log Cake (Yule Log)

This French dessert came from the 1600s. People make this cake to look like a wood log, perfect for Christmas. The chocolate sponge cake gets rolled up with cream filling and chocolate frosting on top. You'll get both great taste and a beautiful centerpiece for your holiday table.

Preparation Time: 40 minutes

Cooking Time: 3 hours

Serving Size: 8

Ingredients:

For the Cake:

- 6 large eggs, separated
- 3/4 cup granulated sugar, divided into 1/2 and 1/4 cup pieces.
- 1/4 teaspoon kosher salt
- 1/2 cup all-purpose flour
- 1/4 cup unsweetened cocoa powder
- Powdered sugar for sprinkling

For the Filling:

- 1&1/4 cups heavy cream
- 1 teaspoon pure vanilla extract
- 1 pinch kosher salt
- 1/4 cup powdered sugar
- 2 teaspoons gelatin (optional)

For the Frosting and Decorating:

- 5 tablespoons cocoa powder
- 1 teaspoon pure vanilla extract
- 3 tablespoons heavy cream
- 1 pinch kosher salt
- 1 stick (1/2 cup) butter, softened
- 1 & 1/2 cups powdered sugar, with additional for garnish.
- Chocolate curls
- Fresh cranberries
- Small rosemary sprigs

Instructions:

a. Heat oven to 350°F. Get a 15x10-inch jelly roll pan ready with parchment paper and cooking spray. Mix the dry stuff for the cake: flour, cocoa powder, and salt in a bowl.
b. In another bowl, beat egg yolks until they get thick.
c. Add 1/2 cup sugar slowly until the mix turns pale. Add the flour mix.
d. Beat egg whites in a clean bowl until soft peaks show up.
e. Add the last 1/4 cup sugar bit by bit until stiff peaks form.
f. Fold this into your cake mix carefully.
g. Spread the mix in your pan evenly and bake for 12 minutes. The top should spring back when you touch it. Put powdered sugar on a clean kitchen towel. Flip the warm cake onto it and take off the paper. Roll it up with the towel from the short end. Let it cool.
h. For the filling: If using gelatin, mix it with 2 tablespoons cold water. Let it sit for 5-10 minutes, then microwave for 10 seconds.
i. Beat the cream, sugar, vanilla, and salt until medium peaks form.
j. Add the melted gelatin if using. Keep cold until needed.
k. Unroll the cool cake. Spread the filling all over.
l. Roll it back up using the towel to help. Put it seam-side down and chill for 1 hour.
m. Make frosting: Beat soft butter, then add sugar and cocoa.
n. Mix in vanilla, cream, and salt until smooth.
o. Cut the ends off the log. Cover with frosting. Add powdered sugar, chocolate curls, cranberries, and rosemary to make it look like a snowy log with mistletoe.

Special Notes:

- Try adding 1/4 teaspoon of instant coffee powder to the cake mix. It makes the chocolate taste even better without making it taste like coffee.
- Want an easier way? Skip the gelatin in the filling and add 2 tablespoons of mascarpone cheese instead. It helps keep the filling firm and adds a nice richness.

30. Clafoutis

This sweet treat comes from France, where people love it for breakfast or dessert. It's a light, fluffy cake filled with cherries that sink into a creamy custard base. Think of it as a pancake that met a pudding and decided to be friends. It's super easy to make and tastes amazing warm or cold.

Preparation Time: 30 minutes

Cooking Time: 45 minutes

Serving Size: 8 servings

Ingredients:

- 2 tablespoons unsalted butter
- 2&1/2 cups cherries, pitted (12 oz)
- 1/2 cup all-purpose flour
- 1/4 teaspoon salt
- 1 teaspoon vanilla extract
- 1/8 teaspoon almond extract
- 3 large eggs
- 1 cup whole or 2% milk
- 1/4 cup heavy cream
- 1/2 cup plus 2 tablespoons granulated sugar, divided
- Powdered sugar for dusting (if you want)

Instructions:

a. Turn your oven on to 375°F. Put a rack in the middle.
b. Get a 10-inch pan that can go in the oven (cast-iron works great). Melt your butter in it over medium heat. If you don't have this kind of pan, just use a 2-quart baking dish and melt the butter in the oven. Make sure the butter coats all sides.
c. Put your cherries in the pan in one layer.
d. Dump everything else (except the 2 tablespoons sugar and powdered sugar) in a blender: eggs, milk, cream, 1/2 cup sugar, flour, salt, and both extracts. Blend until smooth.
e. Pour this mix over your cherries.
f. Bake for 20 minutes. Take it out, sprinkle those 2 tablespoons of sugar on top, then put it back in for another 25-30 minutes. You'll know it's done when it's golden brown and only jiggles a tiny bit. A toothpick stuck in the middle should come out clean.
g. Let it cool for 30 minutes. Dust with powdered sugar if you're feeling fancy. Serve it right from the pan.

Special Notes:

- Try this with different fruits! Plums, peaches, or even blueberries work great. Just make sure they're not too juicy or they'll make the custard runny.
- Pro move: Add a splash of bourbon or rum to the batter - about 1 tablespoon. It gives a nice warmth to the flavor without making it taste like alcohol.

Drinks

31. Classic Mimosa

A mimosa is a simple mix of sparkling wine and orange juice that became famous in Paris in the 1920s. It's now one of the most popular brunch cocktails in the world. You'll love how the sweet orange juice mixes with the fizzy wine to make your morning special.

Preparation Time: 2 minutes

Cooking Time: None needed

Serving Size: 10 servings

Ingredients:

- 1 bottle (25.4 oz) sparkling wine, champagne, cava, or prosecco
- 3 cups orange juice

Instructions:

a. Take a champagne flute glass
b. Pour 2.5 oz of your chosen sparkling wine into the glass
c. Add 2.5 oz of orange juice
d. Serve right away while the bubbles are still fizzy

Special Notes:

- For the best taste, make sure both your sparkling wine and orange juice are well chilled before mixing. Warm mimosas aren't as good!
- Try using fresh-squeezed orange juice instead of store-bought - it makes a big difference. If you want to get fancy, you can also try other citrus juices like grapefruit or blood orange for a twist on the classic.

32. Kir Royale

This French cocktail from Burgundy has been around since the 1900s. People drink it at parties and celebrations because it's simple to make but looks really nice. It's a mix of sweet berry liqueur and sparkling wine that gives you a pretty pink drink. You'll love how the fresh berries make it look extra special.

Preparation Time: 5 minutes

Serving size: 4 drinks

Ingredients:

- 1 bottle (750ml) dry champagne or sparkling wine, chilled
- 4 tablespoons crème de cassis, crème de framboise, or Chambord
- 1/4 cup fresh raspberries (optional)

Instructions:

a. Get 4 champagne flutes ready.
b. Put 1 tablespoon of your chosen berry liqueur in each flute. You can add a bit more if you like it sweeter.
c. If you're using raspberries, drop 3-4 berries into each glass.
d. Slowly pour the cold champagne into each glass until full.
e. Serve right away while the bubbles are still fizzy.

Special Notes:

- Money-saving tip: You don't need to use expensive champagne. A good prosecco or cava works just as well and costs less.
- Try freezing the raspberries beforehand - they'll keep your drink cold without watering it down, and they look pretty too as they slowly sink to the bottom.

33. French 75

Born in Paris during World War I at the New York Bar, this drink got its name from a French 75mm field gun. It hits like the artillery - mixing gin's punch with champagne's sparkle. People love it because it's strong but smooth, perfect for celebrations or fancy parties.

Preparation Time: 5 minutes

Cooking Time: No cooking needed

Serving Size: 1 drink

Ingredients:

- 1 oz gin
- 3 oz champagne (or any sparkling wine)
- 1 lemon twist for garnish
- 5 oz fresh lemon juice
- 5 oz simple syrup

Instructions:

a. Fill your cocktail shaker with ice
b. Pour in the gin, squeeze in the fresh lemon juice, and add the simple syrup
c. Put the lid on tight and shake hard for about 10-15 seconds until it's super cold
d. Grab a champagne flute and strain your mixture into it
e. Now slowly pour in the champagne - it'll fizz up nicely
f. Take a nice piece of lemon peel, twist it over the drink to get those oils out, and pop it in

Special Notes:

- Try using honey syrup instead of simple syrup - it adds a nice richness that works great with the gin
- Keep your champagne flute in the freezer for 15 minutes before making the drink. A frosty glass keeps your cocktail colder longer and looks fancy too.

34. Vin Chaud

This hot spiced wine comes from France where they call it "Vin Chaud". It's perfect when it's cold outside. The mix of wine, citrus, and warm spices makes a drink that will keep you cozy. People love to have it during winter festivals and holiday parties.

Preparation Time: 5 minutes

Cooking Time: 25 minutes

Serving Size: 4 servings

Ingredients:

- 1 bottle (25.4 oz) red wine (merlot, pinot noir, or burgundy)
- 1 whole orange
- 1 whole lemon
- 1-2 cinnamon sticks, plus extra for serving
- 1 whole star anise
- 1 inch fresh ginger, peeled
- 1/8 teaspoon freshly grated nutmeg
- 1/2 cup brown sugar

Instructions:

Clean your orange and lemon well. This is extra important if they're not organic.

Get your orange ready:

a. Take off a few strips of the orange peel (just the orange part, not the white stuff). Save these for later.
b. Cut the rest of the orange into thick slices (about 1/2 inch).

Peel the lemon in long strips. Again, avoid the white part.

Get a large pot and put in:

   a. The orange slices
   b. Lemon peel strips
   c. Wine
   d. Brown sugar
   e. All the spices

Heat it up on medium until you see tiny bubbles, then stir until the sugar melts.

Turn the heat down low and let it warm for 20 minutes. You want to see small bubbles and a bit of steam, but no boiling - this keeps the alcohol and good flavors in.

When done, either:

   a. Pour through a strainer into a clean pot, or
   b. Use a spoon with holes to fish out the orange, spices, and ginger

Keep it warm on very low heat and serve in glasses. Add an orange peel twist and cinnamon stick to each glass.

Special Notes:

- Add 2-3 black peppercorns to the mix - they give a subtle warmth that works really well with the other spices.
- Want it sweeter? You can add honey instead of extra sugar. It adds a nice smooth flavor that goes great with the spices.

35. Pastis

This classic French drink has been a favorite in France since the 1930s. It's a simple mix of Pastis (anise-flavored spirit) and water that turns from clear to cloudy white when mixed. People love it as a cool drink before dinner or during hot summer days.

Preparation Time: 5 minutes

Serving size: 2 servings

Ingredients:

- 5 oz Pastis or Pernod
- 6 oz ice-cold mineral water
- Ice cubes (optional)

Instructions:

a. Pick a tall glass for each serving
b. Pour the Pastis into each glass
c. Add ice cubes if you want (this isn't the traditional way, but it works great on hot days)
d. Slowly pour in the cold water
e. Watch as the drink turns from clear to milky white
f. Add more or less water to make it stronger or lighter - it's up to you

Special Notes:

- Want it fancy? Freeze some star anise in ice cubes beforehand. They look pretty and add more flavor as they melt.
- For a twist, try adding a tiny splash of mint syrup. It's not traditional, but the mix of mint and anise makes a really fresh taste that many people enjoy.

36. Cognac

This drink was born in Paris during World War I at the New York Bar. The drink got its name from the French 75mm field gun because it hits you as hard as the artillery piece! It's a mix of cognac, citrus, and bubbles that's both strong and refreshing.

Preparation Time: 5 minutes

Serving size: 1 drink

Ingredients:

- 2 oz cognac
- 3 oz champagne or sparkling wine
- 5 oz fresh lemon juice
- 25 oz simple syrup
- 1 lemon peel for garnish

Instructions:

a. Fill your cocktail shaker with ice
b. Pour in the cognac, lemon juice, and simple syrup
c. Shake vigorously for 10-15 seconds, or until the shaker feels chilly.
d. Strain the mixture into a champagne coupe or tall glass
e. Top it off with the champagne
f. Take your lemon peel, and squeeze it over the drink to release the oils
g. Drop the peel into the drink

Special Notes:

- Want it extra fancy? Freeze some grapes and use them instead of ice cubes - they'll keep your drink cold without watering it down
- If you're feeling adventurous, try adding a tiny splash (about 0.25 oz) of St-Germain elderflower liqueur - it adds a nice floral touch that works really well with the champagne.

37. Lumiere - A Gin Cocktail

This fancy gin drink comes from a top cocktail bar in New York. It mixes gin with elderflower and green herbs to make something fresh and bright. If you like drinks that aren't too sweet but still taste smooth, you'll love this one. Perfect for spring evenings or fancy dinner parties.

Preparation Time: 5 minutes

Serving size: 2 drinks

Ingredients:

- 5 oz gin
- 75 oz fresh lime juice
- 1 dash orange bitters
- 1 oz St Germain Elderflower Liqueur
- 75 oz green Chartreuse

Instructions:

a. Get your mixing glass ready with some ice cubes.
b. Measure and pour in the gin first.
c. Add the St Germain, then the green Chartreuse.
d. Squeeze in your fresh lime juice.
e. Add just a quick dash of orange bitters.
f. Give everything a good stir until the glass feels cold on the outside.
g. Get your coupe glass nice and chilled.
h. Strain the mix into your cold coupe glass.

Special Notes:

- Keep your coupe glass in the freezer for 10 minutes before making the drink. The extra-cold glass helps keep everything crisp longer.
- Try adding a tiny pinch of sea salt - it brings out the herbal flavors and makes the lime taste even fresher. Don't worry, it won't make the drink salty!

38. Calvados Sidecar

A French spin on the classic Sidecar cocktail, swapping cognac for apple brandy (Calvados). This drink was born in Paris during the 1920s. The mix of sweet, sour, and apple flavors with a hint of cinnamon makes it perfect for fall evenings. It's smooth, not too strong, and tastes like apple pie in a glass.

Preparation Time: 5 minutes

Serving size: 1 drink

Ingredients:

- 1 oz Calvados (French apple brandy)
- 1 wedge of lemon
- 2 tablespoons cinnamon-sugar mix (1 tablespoon each cinnamon and sugar)
- 1 oz Cointreau
- 1 oz fresh lemon juice
- 1 orange peel twist for garnish

Instructions:

a. Mix equal parts cinnamon and sugar on a small plate.
b. Take your lemon wedge and run it around the rim of your cocktail glass.
c. Turn the glass upside down and dip just the edge into the cinnamon-sugar mix. You want a thin, even coating.
d. Put the glass in the freezer - this helps the sugar stick better.
e. Fill your cocktail shaker with ice.
f. Pour in the Calvados, Cointreau, and fresh lemon juice.
g. Shake hard for about 10-15 seconds until the shaker feels ice-cold.
h. Take your glass from the freezer and strain the drink into it.
i. Finish by adding the orange twist on top.

Special Notes:

- Try aging your Calvados-based cocktail in a small oak barrel for 1-2 weeks. This adds woody notes and makes the drink smoother.
- For a more complex flavor, add 2-3 drops of apple bitters or replace the plain cinnamon-sugar rim with one made using dried, ground apple chips mixed with the cinnamon-sugar.

39. Café au Lait

This classic French coffee drink is a mix of hot coffee and warm milk that's super popular in French cafes. It's basically France's version of a latte, but less fancy and more homey. The drink is perfect for people who find regular coffee too strong but still want their morning caffeine fix.

Preparation Time: 5 minutes

Cooking Time: 5 minutes

Serving Size: 1 serving

Ingredients:

- 4 oz (1/2 cup) milk, steamed
- 4 oz (1/2 cup) strong French roast coffee, hot

Instructions:

a. Get your coffee and milk ready. Make sure your coffee is fresh and hot - French roast works best.
b. Steam your milk until it's hot and has a nice foam on top. Keep the foam aside for later.
c. Take a big coffee cup or mug.
d. Pour in the hot coffee first.
e. Add the steamed milk slowly (not the foam yet).
f. Give it a quick stir to mix everything together.
g. Now top it off with the foam you saved from earlier.
h. Serve it right away while it's nice and hot.

Special Notes:

- Want the real French cafe experience? Heat your cup with hot water first, then dump it out before making your drink. This keeps your coffee hot longer.
- No steamer? No problem! Heat your milk in the microwave until hot (about 1 minute), then shake it in a sealed jar for 30 seconds. You'll get a decent foam that works just fine.

40. Hot Chocolate (Chocolat Chaud)

This is the real French hot chocolate - thick, rich, and super chocolatey. It's nothing like the powdered stuff you've had before. Born in Paris's fancy cafes, it's now loved worldwide. With good dark chocolate and cream, you'll make the best hot chocolate you've ever tasted.

Preparation Time: 3 minutes

Cooking Time: 5 minutes

Serving Size: 2 people

Ingredients:

- 8 ounces bittersweet chocolate (70% or higher), chopped
- 1/2 cup heavy cream
- 1&1/2 cups whole milk
- 2 teaspoons powdered sugar
- 1/2 teaspoon espresso powder (optional)
- Whipped cream for serving

Instructions:

a. Pour milk and cream into a medium pot. Add powdered sugar and espresso powder if using.
b. Put the pot on medium heat. Keep whisking until you see tiny bubbles around the edge of the pot. Don't let it boil - you'll know it's ready when the milk starts to steam.
c. Take the pot off the heat. Drop in all your chopped chocolate and stir until it's completely melted. If the chocolate isn't melting fully, put the pot back on low heat for a few seconds.
d. Pour into mugs and top with a big dollop of whipped cream.

Special Notes:

- Try warming your mugs with hot water before pouring in the chocolate. Empty them just before using. This keeps your drink hotter longer.
- Want it even richer? Add a tiny pinch of salt and 1/4 teaspoon of vanilla extract. These bring out the chocolate flavor without making it taste salty or vanilla-y.

Conclusion

We hope these recipes have shown you that French cooking can be both fun and doable. Every great French chef started exactly where you are - learning one recipe at a time, making mistakes, and getting better with practice.

Remember, cooking French food isn't about being perfect. It's about enjoying the process, learning new skills, and sharing good food with people you care about. Some days you might whip up a quick croque monsieur for lunch, other days you might spend a happy afternoon making a chocolate soufflé rise just right. Each time you cook, you'll get more comfortable with these time-tested techniques.

Don't be afraid to make these recipes your own. Maybe you'll add different herbs to your ratatouille, or try a new cheese in your quiche. That's how cooking traditions grow and change. The most important thing is that you're cooking food you love to eat and share.

Keep this book in your kitchen, splatter the pages with sauce, fold down corners of your favorite recipes, and write notes in the margins. A well-used cookbook is a sign of happy cooking and good meals shared.

And remember - French cooking isn't just about the food. It's about taking time to enjoy meals with friends and family, celebrating both everyday moments and special occasions with dishes made with care and love.

Now, go ahead and start cooking. Your kitchen is waiting!

Bon appétit!

Author's Afterthoughts

Thank you for reading my book. Your feedback is important to me. It would be greatly appreciated if you could please take a moment to REVIEW this book on Amazon so that we could make our next version better

Thanks!

Jenny Kings

Printed in Great Britain
by Amazon